SELLING AMERICA

Puns, Language, and Advertising

Michel Monnot
Carleton College

UNIVERSITY
PRESS OF
AMERICA

LANHAM • NEW YORK • LONDON

Copyright © 1981 by

University Press of America,™ Inc.

4720 Boston Way
Lanham, MD 20706

3 Henrietta Street
London WC2E 8LU England

Library of Congress Cataloging in Publication Data

Monnot, Michel.
   Selling America.

   1. Puns and punning. 2. Advertising–Language. I.
Title.
PN6149.P85M66   818'.5402   81–40840
ISBN 0–8191–2002–2   AACR2
ISBN 0–8191–2003–0 (pbk.)

All University Press of America books are produced on acid-free
paper which exceeds the minimum standards set by the National
Historical Publications and Records Commission.

Illus: Picasso's Dora Maar, p. 8, (c) SPADEM, Paris/VAGA, NY

1981

To my father and to
    Vern E. Shuckhart,
    both master punsters.

ACKNOWLEDGEMENTS

I wish to thank all the good people whom I have infected with the disease of pun-collecting, and who have provided me with a copious amount of the material for this book, in particular Laurel Hall, Karen LaViolette, Laura Levison, Edna Loose, Lisa Neal, Gerard Pigeon, Sue Reynolds, Beth Rubin, Naomi Rubin, Marilyn Schuster, and Doris Tuomi; my colleagues Ed Sostek and Ulf Zimmerman, for precious advice on form and content; Julia Marshall for the graphic illustrations; Gene Bauer and Robb Harriss for help with the photography; Katie Mahoney for preparing the typescript; Nikki Lamberty for the typing; Peter Stanley, Dean of Carleton College, for his encouragement and his generous financial assistance; and my wife and children for their patience and forbearance.

Special thanks also to all the companies which have not only provided the puns, but have given me permission to use them in this book. My apologies to all those unidentified creators whose names I was not able to record from billboards while speeding down the highway.

TABLE OF CONTENTS

INTRODUCTION

Pun making, or paronomasia, as it is called in scholarly circles, is a mania. Pun collecting is a disease. In my case, the mania was inherited, the disease acquired. For the last ten years I have made a serious, if not continuous effort (after all some diseases have remission periods) to gather puns. And like most people afflicted with a disease I have tried to find its causes and how it spreads.

My studies, however, clearly had to be limited, because I soon discovered that puns, like germs, are not only innocuous or virulent, friendly or nasty, helpful or detrimental, they are also ubiquitous. The study of the cause and effect of all manners of puns would have been as fruitless as the study of the cause and effect of all manners of germs.

Being a trained linguist rather than a litterateur, I focus my attention on the world of advertising where puns have reached epidemic proportions within the very fiber of American society. Since the late 60's the pun has been sweeping Madison Avenue, and advertising agencies have been playing a game of one-up-manship which finds its expression not only on TV and radio, but also on billboards, in magazines, and in newspapers all over the land.

What reactions do advertisers' puns elicit from potential consumers? In general, they vary between intellectual contempt and slight amusement. These reactions can be explained by the application of kinetic theory in much the same way that Bergson applied it to laughter: just as a spectator watching an action anticipates the next steps ever so minutely, so a reader/listener always slightly anticipates the linguistic chain, be it phonetic, syntactic or semantic. And he does so in a linear manner. For instance, when I tell my children, "Be home at six o'clock for ...", they most likely anticipate that the next sounds will be /s/-/ʌ/-/p/-/ə/-/r/-(supper). They know that these sounds combine into a word functioning in the sentence as a noun, and that this word has both universal and specific meanings. Universally, they know it is an action where food is ingested; specifically, they picture the family dinner table and the various rituals and habits which accompany the scene. All these inferences are done in a linear manner: the /s/ will come before /ʌ/ before /p/ before /ə/ before /r/. The noun will come after the preposition "for," and the images elicited will follow in a logically anticipated chain of events. But when a pun occurs in that chain, the linearity is broken, creating two divergent fields of meaning where the reader/listener expected but one. This breaking of the anticipated line creates a basis for humorous reaction; for example, see Illustration 1.

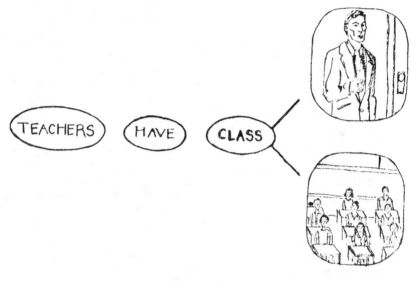

Illus. 1

The ambiguity created by a pun is usually resolved by the reader/listener readily supplying two meanings: one logical, the other often incongruous. Take, for example, the advertisement of Western Airlines, which offers you:

"Three feet for your two legs."

The first logical meaning of "three feet" is that of distance (3') but when further confronted with two legs, the reader/listener cannot fail to react to the incongruity of the image. He has been tricked--or tripped. But he knows it was intentional, and he will react with a smile or a grunt, but one way or another he will react.(Illus. 2)

4

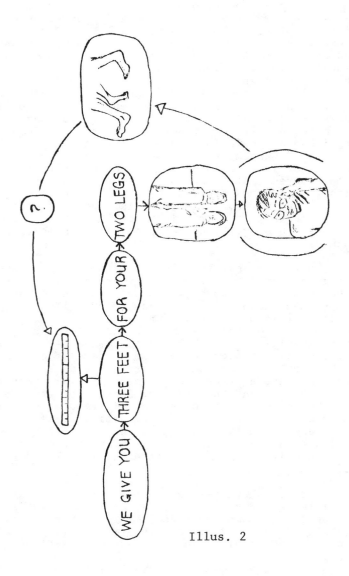

Illus. 2

This reaction to puns is almost always humorous partly because an ambiguous situation has been created. At this point, one may wonder how, in an advanced society such as ours, so many ambiguous situations can arise. Actually, this is a problem common to all languages for the simple reason that there exists an infinity of situational possibilities, but a limited set of linguistic tools and signals to describe them. Any language has a well-determined number of sounds known as phonemes (approximately forty for English), a limited number of words (approximately 90,000 for English), and a limited number of rules which determine the arrangement of those sounds and words (grammar). Nor is this concept limited to modern languages: twenty-three centuries ago, Aristotle wrote to the effect that words are finite and so is the sum total of compound words, while potential human experiences are infinite in number. Inevitably, then, the same words--both single and compound--have a number of meanings.

Most linguists today who try to resolve these ambiguities think of them as a near calamity. It is true that an ambiguous situation is not necessarily always a pleasant one, but puns, especially in advertising, or in most social contexts, strike me as being the opposite of this calamity because they are an intentional form of ambiguity that requires a knowledge of linguistics as well as a spark of creativity. Such intentions are commonplace in our daily experience, and are not restricted to the linguistic chain. They can be found in every art form. For example, J.D. Hubert, a critic of French literature, describes the result created by voluntary ambiguity as "a simultaneous multiplicity of meanings which is no more a flaw than a polyphony in a Bach fugue where one can hear, simultaneously, two different melodies." (Illus. 3).

The art of Picasso was often the embodiment of multiple meanings. Picasso was the great mystifier. In the two examples examined below, we have an illustration of the vitality of his art. From one statement emerges a multitude of images and meanings.

In the first example, Dora Maar exemplifies the duality of statements which became one of Picasso's trademarks: the frontal view separated from and simultaneously incorporated with, the profile view. (Illus. 4).

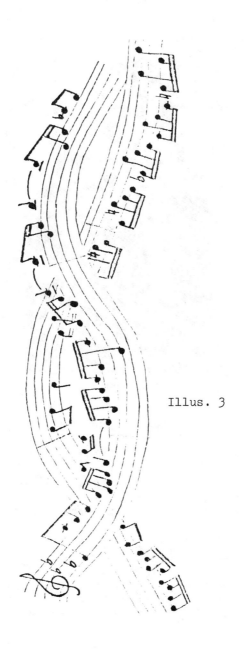

Illus. 3

Illus. 4

In the second example, entitled <u>Journal</u>, one is
confronted by a multiplicity of intents. The word
"Journal" can be seen in two lights. The JOUR represents the aesthetic aspirations of the painter, his
play on, and with, light, and his comment on impres-
sionism. When, on the other hand, the world "Journal"
is considered as a whole, it represents the realistic,
pedestrian, everyday life, the drudgery and the contem-
poraneity of our experiences.

Meanings coming out so freely from a painting or
a drawing remind us of white rabbits coming out of a
magician's hat. The logic is baffled, illusion
replaces reality. We are in the eye of the hurricane,
at the pinnacle of creativity where man, creating a
new order out of chaos, feels his closest bond with
divinity.

I certainly do not want to imply that all puns rival Genesis, but unlike Edwin Newman, with whom I otherwise share the concern for the sorry state of English, I am heartened by what this pun explosion implies for our linguistic patrimony. Granted, some companies use linguistic devices cleverly in order to delude the consumer. But I choose to think that this pervasive use of puns is the illustration that, as a nation, we are involved in a game of linguistic introspection which augurs well for the state of the language. It can also be countered that puns are the lowest form of humor, but I have yet to hear a good argument in that direction. Furthermore, as a language teacher, I see a glimmer of hope. Puns might lead the way in returning us to the basics, for if we can juggle with words, if we can play with them, if we can shift them around to create new meanings that enrich our denatured life and institutions, we will find ourselves, I believe, on a sound track. After all, do we not belong to the Chomsky generation which was fed on the "sound patterns of English"? Puns are like fireworks on a hot summer night: they arise as one, but return to us as many, shedding a strange and warm glow on the darkened landscape.

CHAPTER I

GRAMMATICAL AMBIGUITY:

THE ESSENCE OF THE PUN

Puns function on a variety of levels and use the total spectrum of linguistic possibilities. They may hinge on sound changes, on lexical changes, or on syntactic changes.

Sound changes include either substitution of consonants or vowels, or addition and subtraction of such consonants and vowels. They may also involve changes in more subtle aspects of the phonic chain, such as the displacement of stress and word juncture, as we will see in Chapter 4.

Lexical changes are by far the most common. They produce puns based on the substitution of a single word, or a whole idiomatic expression, as for example, the Yellow Pages ad:
> "Any musician worth fiddling with is in the Yellow Pages,"

or the New York Times':
> "It goes to your head."

See Chapter 2, parts 1, 2, and 3 for more details.

These changes are somewhat superficial in that they do not alter the syntactic composition of the sentence. In other words, a noun remains a noun, a verb a verb, a preposition a preposition. In this chapter, however, I will focus my attention on a deeper level of functioning in which a word can jump across grammatical boundaries. The most striking example in my opinion is a couplet which I found painted in the tunnels of Carleton College:
> "Time flies like an arrow
> Fruit flies like a banana."

I do not want to belabor this readily accessible pun, but I do wish to point out the grammatical ambiguity of the second sentence. Because of the proximity of and the analogy with the first sentence, we are led to think that a fruit flies like a banana, (Illus. 1) until we are struck by the ridiculousness of the situation. At this point, we take one step back, long enough to envisage the second and more logical proposition that fruit flies like bananas. (Illus. 2)

What has happened? In the first sentence we have noun + verb + conjunction:

Illus. 2

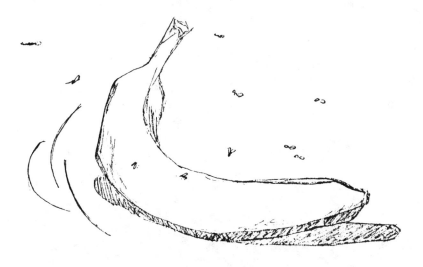

Illus. 2

NOUN		VERB		CONJUNCTION
time	+	flies	+	like

In the second, everything has switched around. The noun is compounded and the conjunction has now become the verb:

NOUN		VERB
Fruit flies	+	like

The next example was alluded to in the preceding chapter. The title of Chomsky's book is an illustration of another grammatical change where "sound" can be interpreted either as an adjective or as a noun:

"The sound pattern of English."

In Houghton Mifflin's:
  "Reading matters,"

we are confronted with the word "matters" which can be understood as a verb (reading does matter) or as a plural noun. Another flagrant example is provided by Teacher's Scotch:
  "Stop. And go light."

15

The whole slogan can be construed as adjective + noun,
as in "red and green light," or as two command verbs
followed by an adverb.

The command verb may turn into a noun as in this
Grain Belt Beer ad:
"Head for the hills,"

or as in Perkins' Restaurants in Minneapolis:
"Steak acclaim," (Illus. 3)

Illus. 3

or into an adjective as in the Yellow Pages ad:
"Open for business." (Illus. 4)

An adjective can become a noun as in this Vogue
ad showing a woman and child in yellow rain slickers.
The caption reads:
"For slicker ideas."

A noun becomes an adverb as in the Yellow Pages
ad:
"Any real estate agent who knows a lot..."

or as in the Simplot Fertilizer ad urging:
"Profit a lot."

A proper noun can become a comparative adjective,
for example, Campbell's Soups':

16

Illus. 4

"V-8.   Makes the bloody merrier."

In this same vein, consider this ad for WCCO in Minneapolis, where the anchor man is Dave Moore:
"Moore people know the score."

Somewhat more risqué again with noun/adjective is this American Dairy Association ad for milk:
"The udder cola."

But the one I prefer in this category is this ad on which listener-sponsored radio stations stake their reputation (or is it "steak"?):
"A rare medium that's always well done."

An adjective can also become an infinitive as in E & J Brandies:
"Makes a rich man pour."

or as in Michelin's ad for steel-belted radial tires:
"We made it first
...We made it last."

A noun changes into a past participle when the John Robert Powers School of Improvement for Women urges its clients to:
"Keep Southern California beautiful: Be Part of the seen."

A past participle as adjective can also find its way into puns. A series of Playboy magazines is depicted on a shelf as:
"Bound to be a classic,"

while the motto of the Heckman book bindery is:
"Bound to please."

A classic in the genre of active vs. passive voice was offered a few years ago by New York Senator Goodell's re-election slogan:
"He is too good to lose."

The possessive case can also be interpreted as a verbal contraction as in:

"Walter Carlo's Bach again."

Noun becomes adverb as in the Yellow Pages:
"Need a beauty salon that styles ahead?..."

Both object and subject can compete for the attention of a verb. Consider Johnny Walker's:
"The gift with nothing to assemble but
special friends."

The double-entendre is caused by understanding: the gift for which you assemble "nothing" (object), and the gift for which "good friends" (subject) assemble. In that same vein one verb can carry unwonted direct objects whose juxtaposition is upsetting enough to make us think twice about the phrase. Consider Jantzen's bathing suit ad:
"Just wear a smile and a Jantzen."

Similarly, wearing one less item...or baring one more, the English Leather lady warns:
"I want my men to wear English Leather or
nothing at all."

Such unusual encounters remind us of Breton's definition of surrealism:
It is the fortuitous encounter, on an
operating table, of an umbrella and a
sewing machine.

All the above cases have been examples of substitution of one grammatical sort for another. A similar effect can be attained through deletion. A classic illustration is offered by a firm which advises us:
"Our business is picking up."

Fine and good, you might say, and remain indifferent until you realize that the advertising firm is the San Fernando Valley Garbage Company. The verb "pick up" then instantly assumes its transitive meaning.

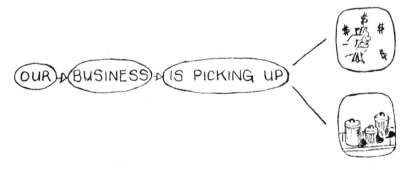

Illus. 5

19

The omission of the direct object is also used by the
Fotomat Company which claims to be:
    "Developing fast."

We're happy for them, but more to the point, we are
happy for ouselves when light shines and we make the
appropriate substitution: "We're developing (photo-
graphs) fast." It clicked again! A third such example is offered by the State of Iowa which advertises:
    "Iowa, a place to grow."

    Similarly, the Yellow Pages offers an example of
deletion, this time not with a direct object but with
the prepositional phrase:
    "Any mover who knows which end is up..."

can be construed as "any mover who knows his stuff,"--
one is tempted to say "who knows the ropes"--but it
can also be envisaged as a sentence where the prepositional phrase would have been deleted as in "any mover
who knows which end of the refrigerator is up..." If
that added information had been explicit, the pun
would have been destroyed through too much precision:
the first meaning would have been eliminated. Nevertheless, we are forced to consider "of the refrigerator" to be there implicitly, because it makes good
sense for a reputable mover to know which end of the
refrigerator is up.

    The final method is that of double deletion. It
is fitting to close this chapter with an ad by a
publishing company specializing in materials for
teaching English as a second language:
    "McGraw Hill is first when English is
    second,"

a clear case of double deletion of the words "place"
and "language."

The following chapters will be devoted to a more
readily accessible analysis of puns. I will attempt
to dissect the surface structure of the puns.

    In the next chapter I examine single words and
idiomatic expressions whose two meanings have the
same spelling and the same pronunciation.

    Chapter III will be the delight or the fury of
spelling bee champions. In it, I present puns which
hinge on the same pronunciation of both meanings but

on different spelling forms.

Chapter IV is devoted to puns whose two meanings
have the same spelling but whose pronunciation is
slightly different. It offers mainly examples of
shift in stress. The accent jumps from one word to
another or from one syllable to another.

Chapter V is bound to provide the majority of
grunt responses. The intention of the punster is
inescapable but the imagination has to be stretched.
In these puns, neither the pronunciation nor the
spelling is the same for both meanings. We find consonant substitution and vowel substitution. This is
bad enough, but wait till we see some puns where a
vowel is substituted for a consonant and vice versa.
Worse yet, we have examples with a mix of consonant/
vowel substitution, and consonant/vowel addition or
subtraction. You cannot say the punster has not tried.

Finally, Chapter VI presents a miscellaneous
batch of three-way puns, of multiple direction puns,
of visual puns, of substitution puns, and, last but
not least, of bilingual puns.

CHAPTER II

SAME SPELLING,

SAME PRONUNCIATION

This Chapter is devoted to words and idiomatic
expressions whose two meanings are rendered by similar sound and spelling realizations. For instance,
the United States Postal Service advertises its zip
code system as:
        "The last word in mail address."

We are familiar with the phrase "the last word in,"
as in "the last word in fashion," "the last word in
design," where the implication is "the ultimate, the
best, the latest," and this is the meaning which first
comes to mind when reading the post office ad. However, in paying closer attention we realize that we
have overlooked a second, more literal meaning. What
is the very last thing (word) written on an address?
The zip code, of course. This particular device may
not be considered humorous but it is an effective
ploy for emphasis.

Part 1. Locutions

The following puns all hinge on an idiomatic
expression yielding two or more meanings. Some are
illustrated, most of them are simply listed.

Author's remark in parentheses.

Air Force: (Illustration 1)

American Bank: (Illustration 2)

American Gas Association:
        "Brule Gas incineration treats pollution
        like dirt."

American Hardware Mutual Insurance: (picture
of a wheelchair):
        "You could get the chair for reckless
        driving."

American Red Cross:
        "Give blood, brothers."

American Safety Council (seat belt sign):
        "Are you putting me on ?"

Armour Ham: (Illustration 3)

Arrow shirts: (picture of Joe Namath sporting
one):

Illus. 1

Illus. 2

"When Arrow made this shirt, it wasn't for any old Joe."

Avis Rent-a-Car:
"Ride Avis out of town."

Baldwin pianos:
"Rent a Baldwin for a song."

Bank of A. Levy:
"Looking for someone you can bank on?"

Bank of A. Levy:
"Our interest in you is guaranteed."

Bayer Aspirin: (Illustration 4)

Best Foods: (picture of a luscious green salad)
"Summer refresher course."

BMW (automobiles and motorcycles):
"Fast company."

Illus. 3

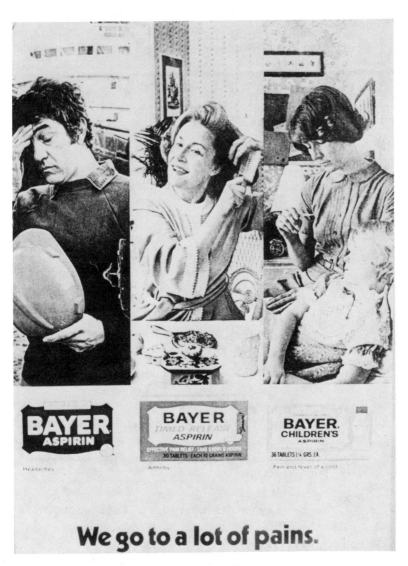

Illus. 4

Burgess batteries:
    "Burgess batteries turn me on."

Burlington Building in New York (textile company):
    "Burlington wants you to go through the Mill."

Caliente Race tracks in Tijuana:
    "Go to the dogs! Caliente!"

Cannon towels:
    "Cannon puts it right on the line."

Capital Plaza Shopping Center in Austin, Texas:
    "Serves you right."

Carbondale, Colorado (coal mining town):
    "We dig it."

Continental Quilt Shoppe:
    "Down with love."

Corday Perfume:
    "Toujours moi: French resistance fighter."
    (It's a killer...or a savior, as the case
    may be.)

Culligan Softwater:
    "Culligan man: look him up in the Yellow
    Pages, under water."

Datsun (cars with doors, trunks and hoods open):
    "How's this for openers?"

Dayton-Hudson, Minneapolis:
    "Allergy-free pillows are nothing to sneeze
    at."

Dayton-Hudson, (Semi-Annual fur sale):
    "Get'm while it's hot."

Dixie Cup:
    "Some people discover Dixie Cups quite by
    accident."

Dupont Chemical:
    "There is a lot of good chemistry between us."

First Federal Savings of San Diego:
    "Bull fighter."

First National City Bank:
    "We work like elephants. For peanuts."

Ford Automobiles:
    "The going thing."

Ford Maverick:
    "It's a little gas."

General Telephone:
    "Hand her an old-fashioned line."

Golden Valley Chrysler Plymouth: (Illustration 5).

Grain Belt Beer:
    "You be the judge--try a case."

Harbor Master: (Illustration 6).

J.B. Hudson, Jewelers, Minneapolis: (Illustration 7).

Icelandic Airlines:
    "A world of difference."

Kodak Cameras:
    "Pick our pocket."

Lejon Vermouth:
    "Automatic dryer."

Libra Cosmetics:
    "Libra won't change color on you."
    (ad in Essence, black magazine).

Lucky Lager Beer:
    "Swallow our pride."

Mail Handlers' Benefit Plan: (Illustration 8).

Mennen: (Illustration 9).

Maurakos candies:
    "They say the sweetest things."

Mexana foot powder:
    "Foot irritation's arch-enemy."

Minneapolis Tribune (health column):
    "Gordon Slovut is good medicine."

31

Bumper Crop

With over 228 brand new 1973 Chryslers and Plymouths we're not trying to squeeze the last dollars out of a deal.

Illus. 5

Illus. 6

Illus. 7

Minneapolis Tribune:
    "This bridge column is a good deal."

Mumm Champagne:
    "It was marzipan, carols, candles, and
    Mumm was the word."

Murray's tobacco: (showing a pipe)
    "Fill an old friend with enjoyment."

NBC News (television):
    "Get a clearer picture."

Nicholson File Co.:
    "There's never a dull moment with Nick."

North Central Airlines: (Illustration 10).

Omaha Race tracks:
    "The most fun in Omaha? You bet."

Pako Posters: (Illustration 11).

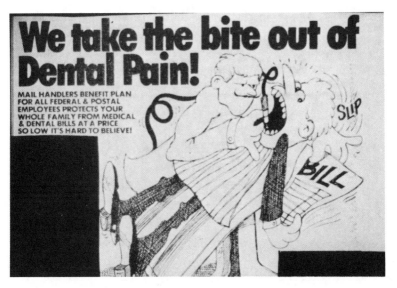

Illus. 8

Papermate (refills with various width tips):
"Is your pen still handing you the same old line?"

Peace Corps:
"French speaking people go far in the Peace Corps. To Africa, for example."

Penthouse (ad for subscription):
"If you're not getting it regularly..."

Poli-Grip Denture Adhesive: (Illustration 12).

Raichle Ski boots:
"Before you sink $145 into a new pair of ski boots you ought to know just what you're getting into."

Richfield, now ARCO, gas company: (showing a gas pump):
"Bargain counter."

Rod Hopp Shows, Inc.: (Illustration 13).

SAAB Automobiles:
    "A well-built Swede to meet all your needs."

San Diego Savings:
    "Fastest draw in the West."

Santa Monica Bank:
    "Put your trust in us."

Schmidt Beer:
    "Workman's Compensation."

Scintilla Silk Sheets:
    "Great in bed."

Schmidt Beer:
    "Make friends with Schmidt."

Shakey's Pizza: (Illustration 14).

Southern California Gas Co.:
    "Don't depend on an old flame."

Super America Gas Stations:
    "A bargain still means a good deal at..."

Illus. 9

STOP DRIVING YOURSELF

FLY NORTH CENTRAL

Don't drive this vacation. Fly and arrive relaxed, enjoy more time there, get back home relaxed too. This summer, let North Central stretch your vacation, make it better than ever fly, don't drive yourself!

Call 612-726-7100 or your travel agent for complete schedule information.

good people make *our* airline great

NORTH CENTRAL AIRLINES

Illus. 10

Blow up someone you love.

Pako Posters $3.95

/filmshops

Illus. 11

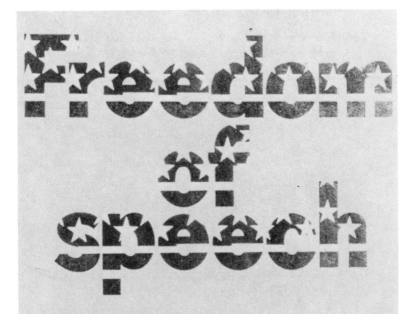

For dentures that ssslip or ssslide.
Poli-Grip, the adhesive that holds so tight,
there's no room for trouble.
No letting go.

POLI-GRIP®

Illus. 12

Teacher's Scotch:
    "Break the ice with..."

Tom Moore soft drinks:
    "Tom Moore leaves you cold."

Toyota:
    "Feel young at 65."

Travel Agency in Barcelona:
    "Go away."

Travel Lodge Int'l Inc.:
    "Rest Easy. There's a Travelodge motel in..."

TreeSweet Products Co.:
    "Only TreeSweet could pull it off."

Tuberculosis and Heart Association:
    "Let's stick together. Use Christmas seals."

University of California at Santa Barbara:
    "Be an athletic supporter. Join the Gaucho
    Gridiron Club."

Illus. 13

Illus. 14

Vassarette Bras:
    "Taking the plunge is what Vassarette is all
    about."

Volkswagen Automobiles:
    "In the end, they're all VW's."

Volkswagen:
    "Twenty-three years getting the bugs out."

Volkswagen:
    "VW relieves gas pains."

WCCO radio in Minneapolis:
    "Channel 4 plays favorites."

Whiskey (the brand name escapes me):
    "You'll like it--we've got the proof."

Yellow Pages:
    "Any answering service that's got the mes-
    sage..."

Yellow Pages:
    "Any bowling alley with room to spare..."

Yellow Pages:
    "Any employment agency that'll put you in your
    place..."

Yellow Pages:
    "Any meat market that won't give you a bum
    steer..."

Yellow Pages:
    "Any radio repairman who won't give you any
    static..."

Yellow Pages:
    "Any sporting goods store with a lot on the
    ball..."

Yellow Pages:
    "Any tailor that'll keep you in stitches..."

Yellow Pages:
    "Shopping center."

Yoplait Yoghurt:
    "Get a taste of French culture."

Zerex:
    "Anti-leak Zerex antifreeze is guaranteed not
    to run out on you."

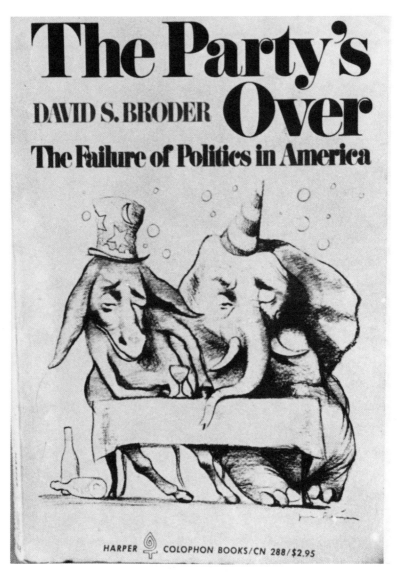

Illus. 15

Part 2. Single Words

In the second part of this Chapter, I present puns which hinge only on a single word. That word may be a noun, an adjective, a preposition, an adverb, or a verb. That word may also jump across these categories. In my opinion a classic example of such puns is Jim Beam's,
"A proud past, a perfect present."
(Illustration 1)

As in the previous subdivision of this Chapter, I present a mixture of puns, some as they originally appeared in the ad, the majority simply listed.

Alcan Building Products:
"The Alcan Plan: Once you know the facts, chances are you'll be siding with us."

Alitalia:
"Swing in the cradle of civilization."

American Cancer Society:
"No butts about it--Stop Smoking."

American Cancer Society:
"The best tip yet? Don't smoke a cigarette."

Arrow Cordials:
"Give your beau an Arrow."

BankAmericard: (Illustration 2).

Bank of America (picture of a check):
"Endorsed by college students."

Bank of Japan:
"Orient yourself to the Bank of Japan."

Black Velvet Whiskey:
"Wrap someone you love in Black Velvet. Give them drums of it."

Carleton College (sign on building entrance):
"Please close this door.
Us college folks value all our degrees."

Chevrolet (walk-in wagon):
"Why stoop to others?"

Chevrolet (Al's used cars):
"Why not break down and get a car that won't?"

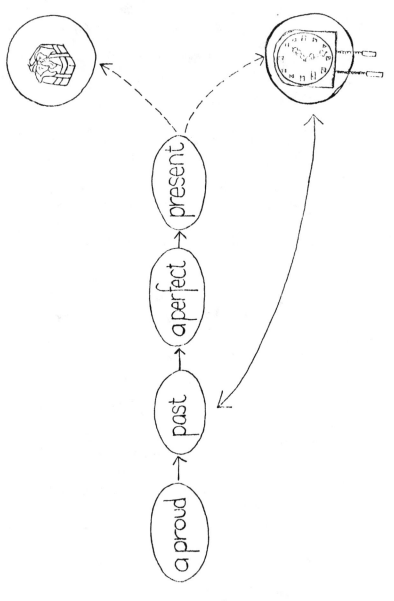

Illus. 1

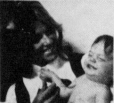

Illus. 2

47

Circus Nuts: (Illustration 3).

Clairol:
     "Don't tangle with Hair-So-New."

Illus. 3

Club cocktails:
   "Nobody makes better cocktails than we can."

Copper Development Association:
   "Copper roofing: nothing tops it."

Cross desk set:
   "Creating a better impression."

Curad:
   "It'll stick with you."

Dansk:
   "Dansk starts a revolution in China."

Dermassage:
   "Get that chap off your knees, lady."

Detroit, Toledo and Irontown Railroad:
   "We have the connections."

Doc's Electric, Inc.: (Illustration 4).

First Federal Savings of Minneapolis:
   "Lick the high cost of mailing (and driving,
   too.)"

Illus. 4

Ford Automobiles:
"When it comes to wagons, nobody swings like
Ford."

Four Roses Whiskey: (Illustration 5).

Illus. 5

General Telephone:
    "Give your kid a hang-up."

General Telephone:
    "Give your wife a new ring."

General Telephone:
    "Keep your rings in a box."

Genesco, Formfit Rogers: (Illustration 6).

Glueck Beer:
    "Glueck-glueck."

Gold Bond Stamps:
    "Thank you from Gold Bond. You rate our
    stamp of approval."

Gould Electric (lights):
    "Brightest gift idea."

Grain Belt Beer: (Illustration 7).

Grain Belt Beer: (Illustration 8).

Hatchcover Restaurant, Madison, Wisconsin:
    "We'll steak our reputation."

Heckman Bindery:
    "Bound to please."

Henredon:
    "Henredon translates from the French...
    beautifully."

Heritage Key ring:
    "Give someone a ring."

Hillcrest:
    "Racqueteers: Get your three days in court
    at our expense."

Holland House Cocktail Mixes:
    "We do wonders for your spirits."

Home Federal Savings:
    "Take more interest in your savings."

M. Hyman and Son (men's clothing store):
    "We suit the big guys."

Be Somebody with Formfit Roge
a division of Genesco

The natural look is busting out all over.

Illus. 6

Illus. 7

Illus. 8

Icelandic Airlines: (Illustration 9).

Jack-in-the-Box (drive-in restaurants):
   "We have a fast turnover."

Illus. 9

Illus. 10

Jacobsen's (clothing store in Northfield, MN):
    "If you need zip, we got zippers."

Jerry Lewis Labor Day Telethon: (Illustration
10).

Jet Propulsion Lab:
    "Live in Pasadena.   Work on the moon."

Kennedy Transmission:
    "Winnie didn't go to Kennedy Transmission.
    Oh!   Pooh!"

Kentucky Fried Chicken:
    "Best legs in town."

Kraft:
    "Away from the roost, think chicken."

Landmark:
    "After you split, strike it rich at the
    Landmark, only a ten-pin away."

Lanvin:
    "Veruschka is a sinner (my sin)."

Litter box:
    "Kitty-a-go-go."

London Times:
    "Our readers are blessed with fine features."

March of Dimes: (Illustration 11).

Illus. 11

Mitchum anti-perspirant:
    "Underarm yourself."

North American Van Lines:
    "Move up the right way."

Northfield Cleaners:
    "If your clothes are not becoming to you,
    you should be coming to us."

Northwestern Banco Banks:
    "Mary Quinn's stocks, bonds and real estate
    no longer keep her awake nights. We have
    her trust."

Norwalk Knives:
    "Norwalk has the edge in knives."

Illus. 12

Old Charter Bourbon: (Illustration 12).

Old Grand-Dad Distillery Co. (showing a marble
bust of the founder):
    "Head of the Bourbon Family."

Olivetti Corporation of America:
    "Duke Ellington at the Key Board."

Olympia Brewing Co.:
    "Cool way to treat warm friends."

Qantas Airlines: (Illustration 13).

Repair Shop (automobile exhaust):
    "Our business is exhausting."

Parliament Cigarettes (picturing London's
Parliament Building):
    "Spend ten days as a guest of Parliament."

Power's Men's Wear:
    "You've got Powers."

Proctor and Gambles:
    "Dishes so shiny you can see yourself in
    them...and that's a nice reflection on
    you."

Promotional device (book of matches):
    "For our matchless friends."

Red Devil, Inc. (tools of high carbon steel):
    "The Devil has quite a temper."

Red Star Rail Express Service:
    "You couldn't express it better."

RKO Tool Company: (Illustration 14).

Roto-Rooter:
    "We couldn't do business without your
    back-up."

Roto-Rooter: (Illustration 15).

Rugby:
    "It takes leather balls to play rugby."

Illus. 13

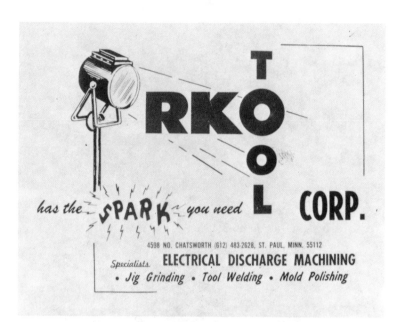

Illus. 14

Illus. 15

Sabena (showing picture of the speaker's wife):
"Shot her on my African trip, old boy."

San Diego Radio Station:
"Catch the Padres."

Schmitt Music Center in Minneapolis:
"The pickin's good at Schmitt's. Pre-
holiday guitar sale."

Schmidt Beer:
"Make friends by the barrel."

Sharp adding machines:
"Business counts on us."

Singing Group of Priests:
"Roamin' Collars."

Southern California Gas Company:
"Over 90% of California swimming pools are
heated with gas because the cost of other
power sources is shocking."

SPCA:
"Don't litter. Neuter your pets."

Suzuki: (motorcycles)
"Express yourself."

Time Magazine:
"Time: Where North American Rockwell puts
space to work."

Toyota Automobiles:
"Toyota gives you a very moving experience."

TreeSweet fruit juice:
"TreeSweet, you fresh thing."

Trojans prophylactics:
"For feeling in love."

WCCO of Minneapolis, Channel 4:
"Television 4 the Great Northwest."

Yellow Pages:
"Any jeweler who can charm you is in the
Yellow Pages."

Yellow Pages:
    "Any Chinese laundry that gets rid of your
    hang-ups..."

Yellow Pages:
    "Any lumber company that pines for you..."

Yellow Pages:
    "Any musician worth fiddling with..."

Yellow Pages:
    "Any pet shop that'll hound you..."

Yellow Pages:
    "Any tailor who'll suit you..."

Yellow Pages:
    "Looking for a photographer who really
    clicks?"

Yellow Pages:
    "Need a printer who's your type?"

Young Quinlan (ad for velvet pantsuit):
    "Evenings are velvet in our dinner suit."

Part 3.   Mixture of Locutions and Words

In the preceding parts of this chapter, I have
shown first how an idiomatic expression can be used
as a pun and then how a word alone can be used as a
pun. The remaining illustrations and examples in this
chapter center on the pun being derived from the mixture of an idiomatic expression and a single word: one
meaning in the sentence is provided by the idiomatic
expression, the other meaning by one of the words in
the sentence. For instance, the American Dairy Association shows us a delicious piece of French bread on
top of which rests a nugget of melting butter. We are
encouraged to:
"Spread the good word."

Upon reading the complete sentence we are immediately
hit by its evangelistic connotation. We scratch our
head for a micro-second and exclaim: "Wait! Something is amiss. This piece of bread with butter on
it has nothing to do with Luke or Mark." But "spread--
ah, yes! spread--spread the butter on the bread! Now
that fits! The word "spread" alone is responsible
for the second meaning of the pun. Q.E.D.

Herewith a few more such gems, either illustrated
or simply listed.

Alcan Building Products:
"Our remote control blind is a shade above
the others."

Bubbling Brown Sugar (name of musical):
"Some like it hot, but everyone loves Sugar."

Cookbook for the Handicapped:
"If you can't stand to cook."

Detroit Free Press:
"Always on top of the news."
(allusion to the Detroit News.)

Germaine Monteil: (Illustration 1).

Garrard (automatic turntables):
"The automatic choice."

Grain Belt Beer:
"Let's put our heads together."

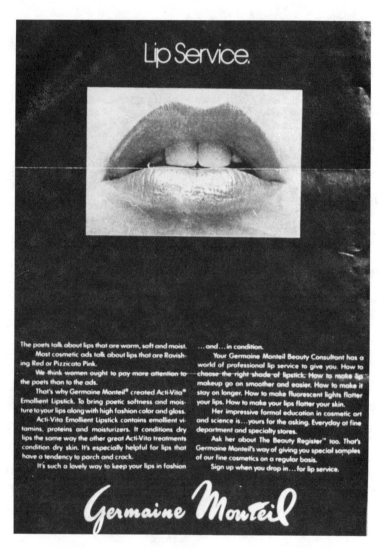

Illus. 1

Minneapolis Bus Co.:
"Take twice a day to relieve congestion."

Pascoe Building Systems: (Illustration 2).

Illus. 2

Republic National Bank of Dallas: (Illustration 3)

Illus. 3

Saloman Bindings:
    "Until now, you couldn't be sure of your
    bindings until you hit the slopes."

Winthrop Laboratories: (picturing Neo-Synephrine
Nasal Spray)
    "We give you breathing room in stuffy
    places."

"Woodsy Owl" of PSC: (Illustration 4).

Illus. 4

CHAPTER III

DIFFERENT SPELLING,

SAME PRONUNCIATION

In the preceding chapter, I had shown how an expression or a word or a mixture of both could produce a pun. The pronunciation and the spelling for both meanings of the pun were identical. In a way we could consider that the collusions of those two meanings, since they had the same phonic and graphic representations, was accidental. A coincidence, an unfortunate coincidence. However, I am prepared to say that since such coincidences are so numerous, since the deliberate intention of creating puns is so obvious, and since I am convinced that we are genuinely interested and amused by word games, these occurrences are by no means coincidences.

In this chapter let us see together how that deliberate intention of creating puns is substantiated. I have said that there are cases when coincidence can no longer be invoked in explaining away a pun. To invoke it would be tantamount to saying that we don't know how to spell. That, to a certain extent, may be the case. But I refuse to believe that people working on Madison Avenue, and marketing products in national advertising campaigns, would make mistakes of pronunciation and spelling. But billboards, magazine ads, T.V., and radio ads are full of those equivocal statements in which the language is distorted one way or the other. The only reason that I can invoke is that we are faced with intentionally produced puns. So the language has been distorted; there has been deterioration in the grammar or in the spelling; some sounds have been shifted around.

In the following pages I focus my attention on puns whose two meanings are carried through identical pronunciation but divergent spellings. Before giving examples drawn from advertising, I'd like to give three such puns taken from other contexts. The first one is the favorite joke of a colleague of mine which he used on dumbfounded students forty years ago at Bemidji State College in Minnesota. Irritated by the lack of response to his literary explanations, he asked the class:
> "Well, in your opinion, what's a metaphor except to keep cows in?"

Bovine-looking students, no doubt. Another favorite of mine is provided by the Christian Campus Crusade labeling its proselytizing fervor as:
> "Prophet sharing."

Then there is a traffic sign near the school in a small community which shows children crossing the road and warns:
> "Dear Crossing."

Most puns offered in this category rely on visual transmission and are found mainly on billboards and in magazines, where they can be read. For instance, when the National Bicycle Week advertises:
> "Give your kids a brake,"

the two meanings do not become apparent until we see the expected "break" written as "brake." The accompanying drawing of a foot stepping on a car pedal makes the second, literal meaning inescapable. The same effect is achieved when the advertising originates from an automobile repair shop:
> "For the brake of your life...
> Frenz Brakes."

American Cancer Society:
> "Help cure cancer. Write now."

Andersen Windowalls:
> "The end of window pains."

Arrow Cordials: (Illustration 1).

Austin Church:
> "Seven days without prayer makes one weak."

Bank:
> "Have Christmas presence."

Barclay's Travelers' Cheques:
> "Wise travelers cheque their cash."

The John Birch Society:
> "Stop Heir pollution. Abolish public schools."

Body Shoppe Sauna:
> "We knead your muscles."

Campari:
> "There is no camparison."

Canon 16:
> "Scuba Scoop, for mocean pictures."

Illus. 1

Chevrolet:
    "America's favorite outdoor grille."

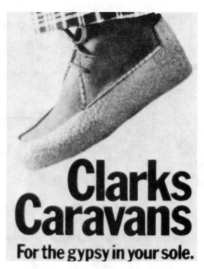

Clarks Caravans
For the gypsy in your sole.

Illus. 2

Clarks Caravans: (see above)

Clothes store in Bemidji:
    "Poise'n Ivy."

Craig Stereo Equipment:
    "Craig is hear."

Dad's Root Beer:
    "When it pours, it reigns."

Book by Russell C. Erb:
    The Common Scents of Smell

Grain Belt Beer:
    "Try one on for sighs."

Grain Belt Beer:
    "The wizard of ahhhhs."

Green Leaf Nursery:
    "Support plant parenthood. Baby your bushes!"

Hancock Shopping Center in Austin, Texas (at
Christmas time):
    "Yule find everything at Hancock Center."

Harrah's antique car collection, Reno, Nevada:
    "Auto sight."

Haskell's Liquor Store, Minneapolis:
    "Haskell's. Largest wine sellers in the
    world."

Hills Brothers Coffee:
    "Head for the Hills."

Jack-in-the-Box:
    "Solves your wait problems."

John Deere: (Illus. 3).

Illus. 3

John Lane Butcher Shop:
    "Happy to meat you."

Johnson Wax Air Freshener:
    "Good sense."

Kodak:
    "Your prints will live happily ever after."

Metropolitan Transport Commission (St. Paul/
Minneapolis):

"Fare Deal."

Minute Maid Orange Juice:
    "We'll give you 50¢ to dessert us."

Mister John's Olympic Hair Fashions:
    "We'll curl up and dye for you."

Northern States Power:
    "Trim your waste."

Northern States Power: (Illustration 4).

Saving Energy Makes Cents.

NSP

Recycled Paper

NORTHERN STATES POWER COMPANY

Illus. 4

National Bike Week:
    "Give them a brake."

Orange Julius at Telegraph Avenue, Berkeley:
    "Gazebo: a garden of eatin'."

Parker Pens:
    "Equal writes for women."

PSA Airlines:
    "PSA routes for your hometown."

74

Pako Photo:
"Prices so low we shutter to think of it."

Philip Morris (showing a broken cigarette):
"America's favorite cigarette break."

Rental Company, Madison, Wisconsin:
"Rentall."

Rockwell International (picture of a drill):
"The hole story."

Rodeway Inns (picture of a lobster):
"Our Maine thing."

San Francisco Civic Auditorium:
"San Francisco Gourmet Faire, Dec. 1-2-3."

Santa Maria Bank:
"We feel loanely."

Saudia Airlines:
"Strong routes make healthy growth."

TEAC's stereo equipment:
"TEAC's new multi-layer decks are the fourmost."

Wellens and Co., Inc. (leasing agency):
"Suite deal for..."

Yellow Pages:
"Any auto shop that will give you a brake is in the Yellow Pages."

Yellow Pages:
"Any baker who kneads the dough..."

Yellow Pages:
"Any bike shop with something to pedal..."

Yellow Pages:
"Any florist with a lot of scents..."

Yellow Pages:
"Any hairdresser who'll dye for you..."

Yellow Pages:
"Any wrecking contractor that'll give you a raze..."

Zimburger, San Francisco:
"Seven days without a Zimburger makes one weak."

Still in the same vein, but this time with the proper noun providing one meaning of the pun, I found the following. I'm always amazed to discover among the numerous representatives of the new generation that the name of the most famous musical group of all times is not being perceived, much less appreciated, as a pun. After all, the leader of the group was the author of a book whose title, John Lennon in His Own Write, was already indicative of what he was going to call his group: a name based on a pun, of course:
"The Beatles."

Creepy if you will, but nevertheless a pun, which personally I find subtle.

Now to more examples.

Brown & Williamson (Kool cigarettes):
"Come up to the kool taste."

Change:
"Send me $18 worth of Change and bill me for $14."

Chicago Tribune (allusion to the Chicago Times):
"A step ahead of the times."

Ebony (allusion to Life magazine):
"Where 2 1/2 million Negro families see their own life."

Ford:
"Kiss Ethyl goodbye. '74 Fords run on regular gas."

Grant's Audio Shop, Minneapolis:
"Grant's Central Station."

Musical group:
"Soul Purpose."

Restaurants in Pasadena (serving hot dogs and beer):
"Frank 'n Stein."

The Viking Press (ad for book by Anita Loos,
Kiss Hollywood Goodbye):
    "Loos talk."

WCCO (television station, Minneapolis, Dave Moore,
anchorman):
    "They're coming back for Moore."

WCCO-TV: (Illustration 5).

Illus. 5

Wright's Silver Cream:
    "Good housekeepers prefer America's #1
     selling silver cleaner, right? Wright!"

Finally these five puns made from compound words:

Jobs:
    "Say Bill Board sent you."

Metropolitan Transport Commission, Minneapolis:
    "The Oughta-Mobile."

Northstar Inn, Minneapolis:
    "Inn comparable."

Olympia Beer:
    "Our sun day best."

Tahiti poster:
    "Tahiti is an Eye-land."

CHAPTER IV

SAME SPELLING,

DIFFERENT PRONUNCIATION

In Chapter II we saw how puns were formed on idiomatic expressions and on words with ambiguous meanings. There was no change of pronunciation and no change of spelling. In this chapter, the puns we encounter are a bit more insidious. The spelling remains the same, the sounds are pronounced the same, but now there is a shift of stress or intonation from one word to another, which produces the dual meaning. We have all heard of foreigners making a mistake by emphasizing the wrong sylla'ble. In these puns it is not a question of the wrong syllable being emphasized, but rather which syllable out of several possibilities will be emphasized. If we stress one, we obtain one meaning; if we stress the other we get a second meaning. To illustrate this shift in stress and into- nation in my own classes, I use the following example made up by Pierre Delattre, my mentor at the Univer- sity of Colorado, and later at the University of California at Santa Barbara:
"What are we having for dinner, mother?"

According to the falling or rising intonation that we place on "mother," we indicate to the listener whether we ask an innocuous question, or one with cannibalis- tic or oedipian overtones. The jolt is unmistakable; students appreciate the example and readily grasp the importance of stress and intonation.

This device is not alien to advertising tycoons and, while my sample collection is not as extensive here as with other forms of puns, I nevertheless deem it impressive. Judge for yourself.

Let's begin by dissecting one example together. T.A.D. Avanti Inc., a company that specializes in automatic answering machines, advertises:
"Find out what people called you."

The following diagram should put things in perspective and reduce the auditory delusion. (Illustration 1).

I like these puns for their subtlety, some so subtle in fact, that I might be accused of finding puns where none were intended.

At any rate in the examples offered below I indicate by an accent mark the two words or syllables which, when alternately emphasized, produce the two desired meanings, and I encourage the reader to try both possibilities out loud. The first choice indi- cates the usual meaning ascribed to the expression;

81

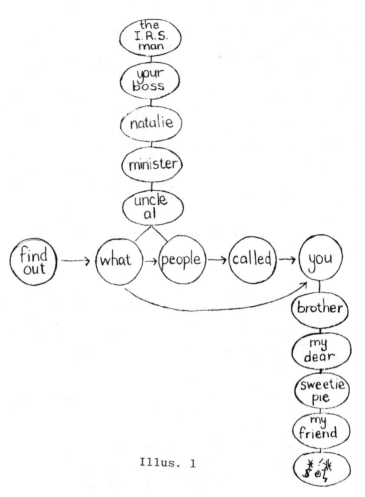

Illus. 1

the second emphasizes an accent shift from which the pun unfolds.

    A & W Root Beer:
        "Tóp Drawer"

        "Top Dráwer"

    American Cancer Society:
        "Cigarette? No Thanks--I can live withóut it."
        "Cigarette? No Thanks--I can líve without it."

American Dairy Association:
    "Everybody needs milk."

    "Every body needs milk."

Arrow Upholstery:
    "Small cover charge."

    "Small cover charge."

Bank (unidentified):
    "Get the picture. Write checks free."

    "Get the picture. Write checks free."

Chicken farm on Artesia Blvd., L.A.:
    "Our chickens are just dying to be eaten."

    "Our chickens are just dying to be eaten."

Coca-Cola: (Illustration 2).

College Inn (student apartment complex in Santa
Barbara):
    "Happiness is having a full house."

    "Happiness is having a full house."

Dart Industries--Tupperware:
    "An airtight case for freshness."

    "An airtight case for freshness."

Dermassage:
    "You've got a fight on your hands."

    "You've got a fight on your hands."

Frontier Hotel, Las Vegas:
    "Put yourself in our place."

    "Put yourself in our place."

Gas Company (shows two burners):
    "Gas shows you where it's at."

    "Gas shows you where it's at."

General Telephone:
    "Smooth talker."

    "Smooth talker."

Glenwood Distilled Water:
    "Covering the water-front since 1884."
    "Covering the water-front since 1884."

Illus. 2

Grain Belt Beer (depicting several pop-tops strung on a chain):
"It works like a charm."

"It works like a charm."

Home Federal Savings, Minneapolis:
"You feel right at Home."

"You feel right at Home."

Merle Norman Cosmetics:
"Are you putting us on?"

"Are you putting us on?"

Neo-Synephrine (booklet about the common cold):
Cold Facts

Cold Facts

Rolling Stone Magazine:
"Shooting Stars: The Rolling Stone Book of Portraits."

"Shooting Stars: The Rolling Stone Book of Portraits."

T.A.D. Avanti: (Illustration 3).

Illus. 3

U.S. Navy:
   "Scholarships available all over the world."

   "Scholar ships available all over the
   world."

Yellow Pages:
   "Best Seller."

   "Best Seller."

Zenith (case with AM and FM):
   "An open-and-shut case."

   "An open-and-shut case."

CHAPTER V

DIFFERENT SPELLING,

DIFFERENT PRONUNCIATION

We now reach a category of puns which can be considered tenuous but for which the intentionality of the punster is undeniable. In the words involved, neither the spelling nor the pronunciation is identical. However, the difference must remain narrow enough to enable the reader/listener to take the leap bridging the two meanings. When Newsweek invites the consumer in the following fashion:

"Having a cerebration? Quote Newsweek,"

we are clearly faced with the intentional triggering of two meanings: that of "thinking" as in cerebration, and that of "feast" as in celebration. The device is insidious, because whether or not we understand the pun, we emerge a winner. In the first case, we say: "Hey, look, they made a mistake," in the second: "Ha, ha, I got your number; I, too, know the big Latin root word." And in both cases we smugly celebrate, with a big inward grin.

Such sound changes vary widely. They may involve a substitution of consonants, as in the example above, they may involve a substitution of vowels, they may involve a mixed substitution of vowels and consonants, or finally, they may simply involve the addition or subtraction of a consonant or a vowel. I must warn the reader here, that this dissection is based on the phonic realization of the puns, not on their spelling realization.

As an easily accessible reference, the phonemic chart on the following page will help the reader. Indeed, when we talk of "vowels" we mean all the vocalic sounds of English, not only the five written ones. The symbols used below and throughout the chapter are those of the International Phonetic Alphabet.

PHONETIC SYMBOLS FOR ENGLISH (INTERNATIONAL PHONETIC ALPHABET)

Consonants

p	ri<u>p</u>
b	ri<u>b</u>
m	ri<u>m</u>
t	sea<u>t</u>
d	see<u>d</u>
n	see<u>n</u>
k	pic<u>k</u>
g	pi<u>g</u>
ŋ	pi<u>ng</u>
f	lea<u>f</u>
v	lea<u>v</u>e
s	cea<u>s</u>e
z	sei<u>z</u>e
ʃ	pre<u>ss</u>ure
ʒ	plea<u>s</u>ure
θ	thi<u>gh</u>
ð	<u>th</u>y
c	<u>ch</u>eap
ʤ	<u>j</u>eep
h	<u>h</u>eap
l	<u>l</u>eap
r	<u>r</u>eap
j	<u>y</u>et
w	<u>w</u>et

Vowels

i		f<u>ee</u>l
I		f<u>i</u>ll
u		f<u>oo</u>l
ʊ		f<u>u</u>ll
e, eI		f<u>ai</u>l
ɛ		f<u>e</u>ll
o		f<u>oa</u>l
ɔ		f<u>a</u>ll
æ		f<u>a</u>t
ɑ		f<u>ar</u>
ə		f<u>ur</u>nace
ʌ		f<u>u</u>n
aʊ		f<u>ou</u>l
aI		f<u>i</u>le
ɔI		f<u>oi</u>l

90

Part 1. Substitution of Consonant

A & W Rootbeer:
    "Foam sweet foam."
    substitution: /f/ for /h/

Bridgeman's Ice Cream:
    "King of the Fountain."
    substitution: /f/ for /m/

British Columbia:
    "The fun never sets in beautiful B.C."
    substitution: /f/ for /s/

Brookline Trust:
    "Start something with your wife ...(a joint
    checking account)."
    substitution: /w/ for /l/

Bumper Sticker:
    "Don't METH around. Speed kills."
    substitution: /θ/ for /s/

Bumper Sticker:
    "Bumper snicker."
    substitution: /n/ for /t/

California Avocado Advisory Board:
    "Avocado and the onion: love at first bite."
    substitution: /b/ for /s/

Chiffon paper towels:
    "A towel for all reasons."
    substitution: /r/ for /s/

Dodge trucks:
    "Dodge trucks are ram tough."
    substitution: /r/ for /d/

Electric Company ad:
    "Air condition electrically. Why fry by
    night?"
    substitution: /r/ for /l/

Four Roses Whiskey:
    "Four Roses Premium Whiskey...and to all a
    good light."
    substitution: /l/ for /n/

Gilbey's Gin; Dry Boisier Vermouth:

"We never stop drying."
substitution: /d/ for /t/

Illus. 1

Gordon's Gin: (Illustration 1).
substitution: /dg/ for /tʃ /

Grain Belt Beer:
    "Thirst sign of spring."
        substitution: /θ/ for /f/

Grain Belt Beer: (Illustration 2).
        substitution: /θ/ for /f/

Illus. 2

Hunting World (bracelet):
    "Knots of luck."
        substitution: /n/ for /l/

Interior Decorating Shop:
    "Everything your hearth desires."
        substitution: /θ/ for /t/

Interwoven: (Illustration 3).
        substitution: /s/ for /ʃ/

Jack Lalanne Gymnasium:
    "Put on your funday best."
        substitution: /f/ for /s/

Kellogg Rice Krispies Cereal:
    "Get on the Rice Side."
        substitution: /s/ for /t/

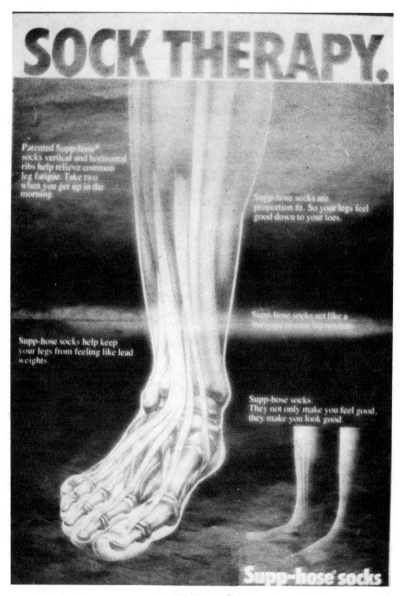

Illus. 3

Kentucky Fried Chicken:
        "Try us on for thighs."
        substitution: /θ/ for /s/

Mappin:
        "Spread a little mappiness this Christmas."
        substitution: /m/ for /h/

Mitchell, Martha (book title):
        The Mouth that Roared
        substitution: /θ/ for /s/

Mythopoeic Society (society's publication)
        "Mythprint; mything link."
        substitution: /θ/ for /s/

Newsweek:
        "Having a cerebration? Quote Newsweek."
        substitution: /r/ for /l/

Parker Pens:
        "Big Red writes again."
        substitution: /t/ for /d/

Pier 66:
        "Let the fun shine in."
        substitution: /f/ for /s/

Politician's re-election slogan:
        "One good term deserves another."
        substitution: /m/ for /n/

PPG Glass:
        "Living with glass in Iowa."
        substitution: /g/ for /k/

Schmidt Beer:
        "Rhapsody in brew."
        substitution: /r/ for /l/

Schwepps soda water:
        "It schwept the whole country."
        substitution: /ʃ/ for /s/

Squirt: (Illustration 4).
        substitution: /t/ for /h/

Stanley Tools (plane):
        "Time shaver."
        substitution: /ʃ/ for /s/

Illus. 4

STP Corporation:
    "The racer's edge."
      substitution: /s/ for /z/

Unidentified:
    "Every litter bit hurts."
      substitution: /r/ for /l/

The Wrestler (film): (Illustration 5).
      substitution: /m/ for /n/

Illus. 5

Part 2. Substitution of Vowels

Air Force:
   "Air Force. Have a great vocation."
   substitution: /o/ for /e/

Anheuser Busch Beer:
   "Our lightest addition."
   substitution: /aI/ for /e/

Band Name:
   "Harper's Bizarre."
   substitution: /I/ for /ə/

BSR turntables:
   "We gave our best turntables the shift."
   substitution: /I/ for /æ/

Colt 45 Malt Liquor:
   "Six appeal."
   substitution: /I/ for /ɛ/

Finnish Cheeses:
   "Swiss cheese from Finland--it's Finntastic."
   substitution: /I/ for /æ/

Grain Belt Beer:
   "Graduate skol."
   substitution: /o/ for /u/

Green Giant: (Illustration 6).
   substitution: /ʌ/ for /ɛ/

Hill & Hill Liquor:
   "Tell your boss to go to Hill."
   substitution: /I/ for /ɛ/

Johnnie Walker Red Scotch:
   "The lick of the Scotch."
   substitution: /I/ for /ʌ/

McLuhan/Fiore book title:
   The Medium is the Massage
   substitution: /ə/ for /ɛ/

Metropolitan Transport Commission, Minneapolis:
   "It's a dime good deal."
   substitution: /aI/ for /æ/

**Good.
Butter.
Best.**

Frozen vegetables you cook
in butter sauce, not water.

Illus. 6

Norelco Pocket Memo (cassette tape-recorder):
"The best way to 'talk' notes."
substitution: /ɔ/ for /e/

Schenley's: (Illustration 7).
substitution: /a/ for /ɛ/

Seven-Up:
"Seven-Up. Right Un."
substitution: /ʌ/ for /ɔ/

Smith's Transfer Corp.:
"The haulmark of service."
substitution: /ɔ/ for /ɑ/

Ventura Luggage:
"For gracious leaving."
substitution: /i/ for /I/

Wine-art:
"The beer essentials."
substitution: /i/ for /ɛ/

Illus. 7

Part 3. Mixture of Consonant and Vowel

American Dairy Association:
"Eat-and-run meals. Do they run in your
family?"
subtitution: /i/ for /hI/

Capital National Bank:
"Losing the battle of the buck?
Our fiscal fitness program can help."
substitution: /s/ for /zI/

Car Care Council:
"Check well before using."
substitution: /tʃɛ/ for /ʃe/

Chris' and Pitt's: (Illustration 8).
substitution: /rI/ for /ər/

General Telephone:
"The trimline phone."
substitution: /trI/ for /stri/

Holiday Inn, Barstow., California:
"Try our seafood. Just for the halibut."
substitution: /hælIbʌt/ for /hɛləvIt/

CALIFORNIA'S NO. 1
GRILL FRIEND

Chris' & Pitt's, the sassy sauces to
make your barbecues remembered!
Now in five brilliant flavors: Garlic,
Onion Bits, Hickory, Hot or Regular.

Illus. 8

103

Kamchatka Vodka:
"Lime juice without Kamchatka is a vodka gimmick."
substitution: /Ik/ for /lɛt/

Norelco Cassette Recorder:
"Ready, Cassette, go."
substitution: /kə/ for /gɛt/

Schaeffer, Francis A. (book title):
Escape for Reason
substitution: /ri/ for /prI/

Seven-Up:
"Don't be left out in the cola."
substitution: /a/ for /d/

Sony:
"Sony. You never heard it so good."
substitution: /ər/ for /æ/

Southdale Shopping Center in Minneapolis:
"Snow place like Southdale."
substitution: /sn/ for /n/

Illus. 9

Sylvania: (Illustration 9).
substitution: /dɔ/ for /ðæ/

104

Part 4. Various Additions,

Subtractions, Substitutions

AAA:
"Discover America. It's 3000 smiles wide."
subtraction: /sm/--→/m/

Acco Graphite:
"Fact. Not friction."
subtraction: /fr/--→/f/

Aurora toilet paper:
"There are two sides to every tissue."
subtraction: /tI/--→/I/

Century Gaslight: (Illustration 10).
substitution: /lo/ for /o/

Clark Store:
"Everything for hue."
subtraction: /hj/--→/j/

General Electric light bulbs:
"We couldn't glare less."
substitution: /gl/for /k/

Grain Belt Beer:
"Make a supreme quart decision."
subtraction: /kw/--→/k/

Hash Dandruff Remover:
"Fight hair pollution."
subtraction: /hɛ/--→ /ɛ/

Health's Angels: (Illustration 11)
substitution: /lθ/ for /l/

Heinz Ketchup:
"It's slow good."
subtraction: /sl/--→/s/

Holland House Cocktail Mixes:
"Sip into something exotic."
addition: /s/--→/sl/

Illinois State Lottery:
"PLAYDAY could make you rich."
subtraction: /pl/--→/p/

Illus. 10

106

Ride with the Health's Angels September 15.

Illus. 11

Kawasaki Motorcycles:
    "More smiles per gallon."
    subtraction: /sm/--→/m/

Lady Schick Electric Shaver:
    "It wouldn't hurt a thigh."
    substitution: /θ/ for /fl/

Levenson, Sam (book title):
    <u>In One Era and Out the Other</u>
    subtraction: /rʌ/--→/r/

Liemmand's Men's Wear:
    "Johnny Carson goes to blazers fashionably."
    subtraction: /ər/--→/ə/

Lycra:
    "If you are positively thigh-catching in
    pants..."
    subtraction: /θai/--→/ai/

Maverill stapler:
    "Goodbye, Mr. Clips."
    substitution: /kl/ for /tʃ/

Minnesota State Fair: (Illustration 12).
    substitution: /ə/ for /æ nə/

New York State Lottery:
    "If at first you don't succeed, buy, buy,
    again."
    substitution: /b/ for /tr/

Norelco (showing products for Christmas):
    "Noelco"
    addition: /o/--→/or/

Oro Bread Co.:
    "Oro d'oeuvres."
    subtraction: /ro/--→/r/

Owatonna Bank:
    "The Loan Arranger."
    subtraction: /ər/--→/r/

Parker Pens:
    "You reporters will be caught with your pens
    down."
    addition: /n/--→/nt/

Illus. 12

Illus. 13

Old Gold: (see above)
      addition: /t/--→ /st/

Richfield (now ARCO):
    "Powerfuel ."
    subtraction: /jʊ/--→/u/

San Diego Federal Savings:
    "Save for a brainy day.   Higher earning...
    higher learning."
    subtraction: /br/--→/r/

Schilling Spices:
    "Schilling gourmet paprika. Worth shaking."
    subtraction: /wə/--→/ə/

Sego (diet beverage):
    "Instant SEGO.   Will-powder."
    subtraction: /də/--→/ə/

Shoe Store in Minneapolis-St. Paul:
    "Tie it, you'll like it."
    addition: /t/--→/tr/

Shoe Store in Minneapolis-St. Paul:
    "Tie one on."
    addition: /t/--→/tr/

Ski Utah poster:
    "Greatest snow on earth."
    substitution: /sn/ for /ʃ/

Skippy Peanut Butter:
    "Swallow the leader."
    substitution: /sw/ for /f/

Slender Diet Soda:
    "Give your family Slender loving care."
    substitution: /sl/ for /t/

Southwest Fidelity Bank:
    "A breath of fresh care."
    subtraction: /kɛ/--→/ɛ/

Tuberculosis and Respiratory Association:
    "It's a matter of life and breath."
    substitution: /br/ for /d/

Unidentified Business School:
    "Earn, baby, earn."
    addition: /ə/--→/bə/

110

Unidentified Restaurant ad:
"Shrimply delicious."
substitution: /ʃr/ for /s/

Western Exterminator Co., L.A.:
"Ants? Give us a crawl today.'
subtraction: /kr/---> /k/

Win Stephens: (Illustration 14).
addition: /s/---> /st/

Women's Army Corps:
"Let yourself grow."
subtraction: /gr/---> /g/

Zorro, The Erotic Adventures of, (film):
(Illustration 13).
substitution: /s/ for /rz/

Illus. 13

It's the lease we can do.

If it's available, we can LEASE (or RENT) it. And on terms that you or your company can live with. Any make or model of car or truck sold in the U.S. Our business is helping your business. It's the lease we can do.

Win Stephens Leasing Co.

south of Wayzata Blvd. on highway 100. Minneapolis Dial the Lease Line 929-0061

Illus. 14

CHAPTER VI

MISCELLANEOUS CATEGORIES

In this final chapter, I have lumped together various categories of puns which occur only rarely, but which could not be left out of this compendium. They include syllabic or word substitution, inversion, multiple direction, combinations of all the factors we have seen in preceding chapters, visual puns, three-way puns, and finally a sort to which I am partial because it provided me with a great deal of entertainment while I was learning English: bilingual puns.

Part 1.   Syllabic and Word Substitution

Bowling alley:
"We're using electricity spare-ingly."

Ebony:
"We're dreaming of a black Christmas."

Ewe's milk cheese:
"It's Ewe-nique."

Kamchatka Vodka:
"Tomato juice without Kamchatka is a bloody shame."

Mitchum anti-perspirant:
"Underarm yourself."

National Biscuit Premium Crackers:
"There's more to Premium than meets the ears."

Samsonite Luggage: (Illustration 1).

Snacks for dogs:
"Lolli-pups."

Part 2.   Inversion

Dermassage:
"Feed the hand that bites you."

Hart Mobile Homes:
"Hart is where your home is."

Illus. 1

Finn's Cameras: (Illustration 2).

Illus. 2

Fleischman's Yeast:
    "Fleischman's Yeast...It lets you bake from
    scratch...Whenever you get the itch."

Nestle's Quik:
    "You can't drink it slow if it's Quik."

Noxema Shaving Cream:
    "Let Noxema cream your face so the razor
    won't."

Oregon State:
    "Relax in a State of Excitement."

Part 4.   Combinations

In the following example:
> "Nurse Mates brings fashion to a uniform world,"

we have an ad with two puns, one on nurse-mate (nurse-maid) and one on uniform (as both adjective and noun). In a Zee toilet paper ad:
> "Say hello to a good buy,"

we have a spelling pun on good buy (good-bye) and an antithesis between this second meaning and hello. In Fordor travel guides:
> "A good buy to fare well,"

we have two spelling puns (good-bye and farewell as a noun) producing an upsetting homonymy.

I'm sorry that for the last example in this category I cannot cite the name of the company that came up with it. Due to an oversight on my part in collecting the pun I forgot to jot it down. At any rate, the ad is a jewel of intricacy and has kept me laughing...or in stitches. The things advertised are pocket patches called Rumper Stitches, an obvious parody of bumper stickers. The company marketing them urges us to:
> "Darn those sew and sews."

Part 5.   Three-Way Puns

Rather than tediously elaborating--I agree that there is nothing worse than a pun needing explanation--I will leave the reader free to interpret the next three examples as he or she wishes. But surely the various meanings will not fail to unfold as a bud into a rose blossoms.

American Red Cross:
> "Give blood, brothers."

Barber shop:
> "Al's Clip Joint."

Iowa State:
> "Iowa, a place to grow."

Part 6. Visual Puns

All the following examples require that one of
the meanings of the pun be carried through or corro-
borated by a visual or graphic representation. They
cannot be transmitted orally. A pharmacy in Chats-
worth, South Dakota, advises us of its:
"Rxeptional service."

The State of Maine whose postal abbreviation is ME
encourages us, for our winter pleasure, to:
"Ski ME."

Volkswagon has provided us many smiles with the:
"L♡vebugs."

A few years ago, an unidentified airline offered:
"We'll fly you to Miami and baɔk."

The duplicating services at Carleton College supplied
an original twist with:
"Duplicating

Duplicating

Duplicating

Hey, look us over."

I have saved the two best ones for personal reasons.
First, I have a very deep sentimental attachment to
Minnesota where I spent the last year of my high
school career as an A.F.S. student, and I cannot but
agree with the Grain Belt Beer ad which, transforming
a beer stein into the shape of the state, proclaims:
"The best things in life are here."

Second, I am partial to my home country and the civilization which, in centuries past, radiated from it,
even though some aspects of that culture come back to
us on occasion as an ironical twist of fortune. This
Levi's ad, produced for French consumers, affords a
perfect illustration thereof. The picture is composed
in such a way as to be an evident replica of Rude's
famous sculpture which, viewed from the Champs Elysées,
adorns the right side of the Arc de Triomph (Illustration 3). It also affords a logical transition
into my last subdivision, that of bilingual puns.

Illus. 3

Part 7. Bilingual Puns

After having taught French in the U.S. for twenty years, I have acquired a substantial collection of bilingual gems which perhaps will find their rightful place in some future endeavor. For the time being, I would like to share another personal experience.

My father, who knows virtually no English, came to visit me one summer in Boulder, Colorado. It was a hot, dry, and windy summer. One afternoon he came home laughing, saying: You'll never guess what I saw. I was walking past a used car lot and many of the cars bore quite appropriate signs but in each case the sign had a spelling mistake in it." The sign to which he specifically referred said "For Sale," which of course he had reinterpreted into the French as "Fort Sale" where the "t" is silent and which means, "very dirty."

Collected from advertising are the following:

Planter's Peanuts showing a tray of succulent hors d'oeuvres, announces:
        "Tray magnifique."

Arctic Cat Snowmobiles invite us in a half-hearted
manner to:
> "Come see, comme sigh."

And finally, concise and classical in its approach,
a Canadian Beer calls itself:
> "Moosehead."*

*"Mousse" in French is pronounced approximately as
"moose," and means "foam" or "head" on a glass of
beer.

ABOUT THE AUTHOR:

Born in Digoin, France, 1940. An AFS scholarship brought him to this country in 1957. He then received his B.A. from St. Cloud State College, MN, and his M.A. in French Literature and Linguistics from the University of Colorado at Boulder. After five years spent as an Associate in Research at the Speech Synthesis Project of the University of California at Santa Barbara under the direction of Pierre Delattre, he received his Ph.D. in French Linguistics from that institution.

Since 1971, he has been teaching French and Phonetics at Carleton College where he is Associate Professor and Coordinator of the College's programs in Pau, France. During the academic year he resides in North-field, Minnesota, with his wife and children, and he spends his summers at a farm house in Southern Burgundy directing bicycle tours of the province for American High School students.